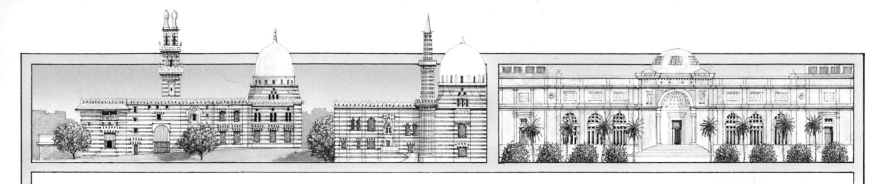

CITYMAZE!

A Collection of Amazing City Mazes

by WENDY MADGWICK

illustrated by DAN COURTNEY, NICK GIBBARD,
DEAN ENTWISTLE AND JOHN FOX

THE MILLBROOK PRESS, INC.
BROOKFIELD, CONNECTICUT

A TEMPLAR BOOK

Published in the United States in 1995 by The Millbrook Press, Inc.
2 Old New Milford Road, Brookfield, CT 06804

Devised and produced by The Templar Company plc
Pippbrook Mill, London Road, Dorking, Surrey RH4 1JE, Great Britain

Copyright © 1994 by The Templar Company plc

Author Wendy Madgwick
Designer Janie Louise Hunt
Consultant Dr Andrew Tatham,
Keeper, Royal Geographical Society, London, Great Britain

Note: The maps of the cities depicted in this book
have been greatly simplified, and only the major roads and buildings are shown.

Madgwick, Wendy, 1946 –
Citymaze! : a collection of amazing citymazes / by Wendy Madgwick
: illustrated by Dan Courtney, Nick Gibbard, Dean Entwistle and John Fox.
p. cm.
ISBN 1-56294-561-0 (lib. bdg.) ISBN 1-56294-846-6 (pbk)
1. Geographical recreations — Juvenile literature. 2. Maze
puzzles — Juvenile literature. [1.Geographical recreations.
2. Maze puzzles. 3. Puzzles] I. Courtney, Dan, ill. II. Gibbard, Nick, ill.
III. Entwistle, Dean, ill. IV. Fox, John ill. V. Title.
GV1485. M33   1994
793.73 — dc20
94–26291   CIP   AC

Acknowledgments: The Templar Company would like to thank the
following organizations for supplying reference material used in the compilation of
these maps: Audience Planners, Australian High Commission, Egyptian Tourist Board,
High Commission of India, Tony Morrison, Joyce and Bob Pope, Lifefile Photographic Agency,
New South Wales Tourist Board, Dr. Bradnock, editor of South Asian Handbook, School of Oriental
and African Studies, Turkish Embassy, Turkish Tourist Board.

Printed in Hong Kong

FINDING THE WAY

Take a tour around the world and visit some of our most beautiful and famous cities. Each city is set in a different country, from the ancient Forbidden City of Beijing in China to the modern cosmopolitan American city of New York. Help guide a group of tourists around central Sydney avoiding all the blocked roads, one-way systems, and hazards. Or find your way in a taxi cab from Victoria Station to St. James's Palace in London. As you trace the correct path through the maze, you'll pass many famous sights. But take care, only one path provides a clear route to your destination—the wrong path could lead to trouble and a dead end.

All the solutions to the mazes can be found at the back of the book, where you'll also find information about the cities and buildings pictured.

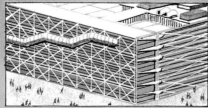
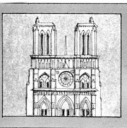
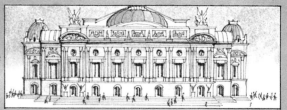

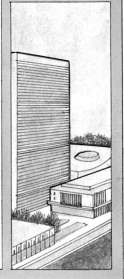

NEW YORK • NEW YORK

New York, the largest city in the United States, is full of amazing contrasts. Manhattan, with its wealth of skyscrapers, bright lights, and noisy traffic jams, is often called simply "the city." The fashionable shops of Fifth Avenue, the business center and stock market of Wall Street, the splendid apartments of Park Avenue, as well as the Broadway theaters and the concerts and sporting events in Madison Square Garden, encourage tourists and businesspeople to flock there in the thousands. But it is not always an easy task to find your way around this hive of activity.

A businessman arriving at Grand Central Station (**A**) decides to take one of the famous yellow cabs to see the Empire State Building (**B**) before he visits the Stock Exchange on Wall Street. He is amazed to find that the route is far from straightforward.

The taxi driver has to overcome many problems — a fire, an accident, a large parade, and a demonstration, as well as the usual traffic jams and "no entry" signs. He has great difficulty finding a clear way through with no obstacles. Follow the roads and see if you can make your way from Grand Central to the Empire State Building. But take care, there are many hazards to negotiate, and only one path is a clear route.

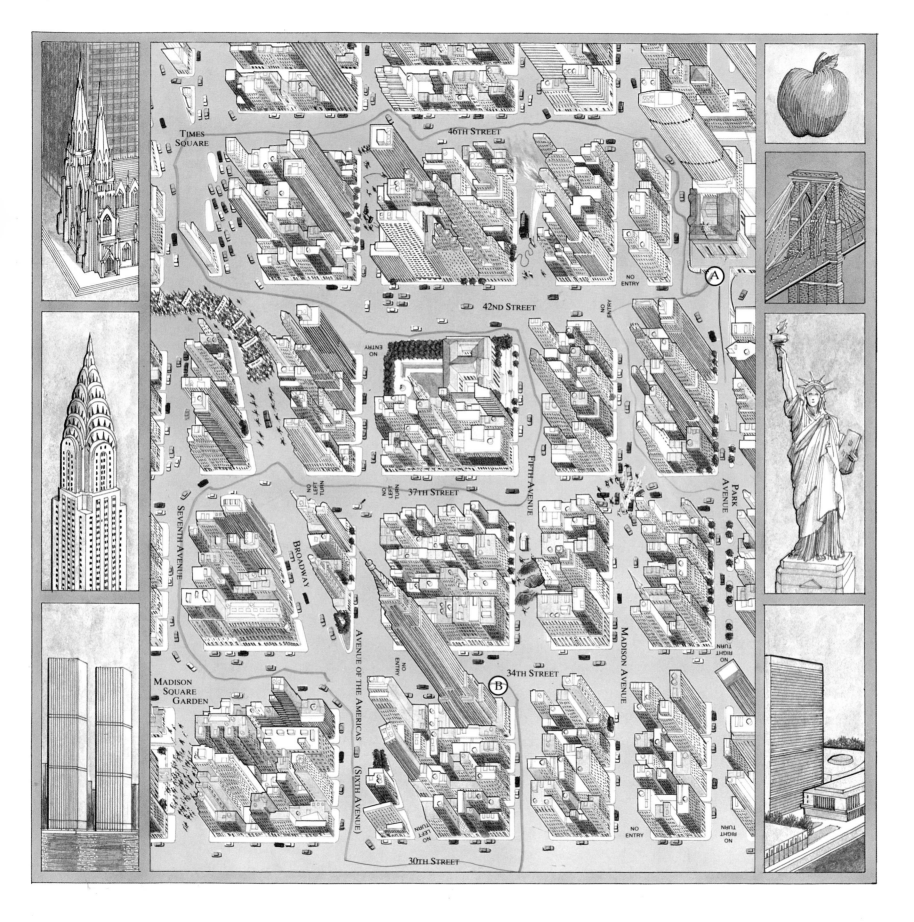

TIMES
SQUARE

46TH STREET

NO
ENTRY

42ND STREET

NO
ENTRY

(A)

NO
ENTRY

FIFTH AVENUE

PARK AVENUE

NO LEFT
TURN

NO
LEFT
TURN

37TH STREET

SEVENTH AVENUE

BROADWAY

NO
RIGHT
TURN

MADISON AVENUE

NO
ENTRY

MADISON
SQUARE
GARDEN

AVENUE OF THE AMERICAS
(SIXTH AVENUE)

34TH STREET

(B)

NO
RIGHT
TURN

NO
LEFT
TURN

NO
ENTRY

NO
ENTRY

NO
RIGHT
TURN

30TH STREET

BEIJING • THE FORBIDDEN CITY

At the center of the walled city of Beijing, the capital of China, lies the moated Forbidden City, or Gugong, with its ancient Imperial Palaces hidden behind a 33-foot-(10-m-) high red-colored wall. From the early 1400s to the beginning of the 1900s, these formed the emperor's court from which ordinary people were excluded on pain of death. Within the royal complex lie enormous squares and gardens with 800 ancient buildings and more than 9,000 different rooms. The broad straight streets of the main city, which center on Tiananmen Square and the Forbidden City, are thronged with bicycles, buses, and people. But nothing can reduce the majesty of the cluster of classically beautiful wooden Chinese buildings with their golden-yellow tiled roofs. Beijing has expanded greatly in the past 50 years and is now a sprawling modern industrial trading center, but the ancient city has been restored and preserved as a monument to its people and is now a museum open to the public.

A group of tourists are being taken on a guided walk starting from the Hall of Supreme Harmony (**A**) back to the courtyard at the entrance to the Bridge across the Golden Water River (**B**). Their guide promises them they will visit many of the most famous sights in the Forbidden City.

Can you find the one clear pathway that the group took?

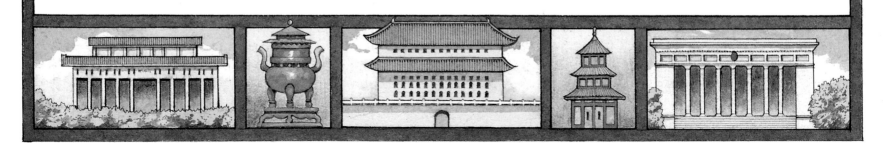

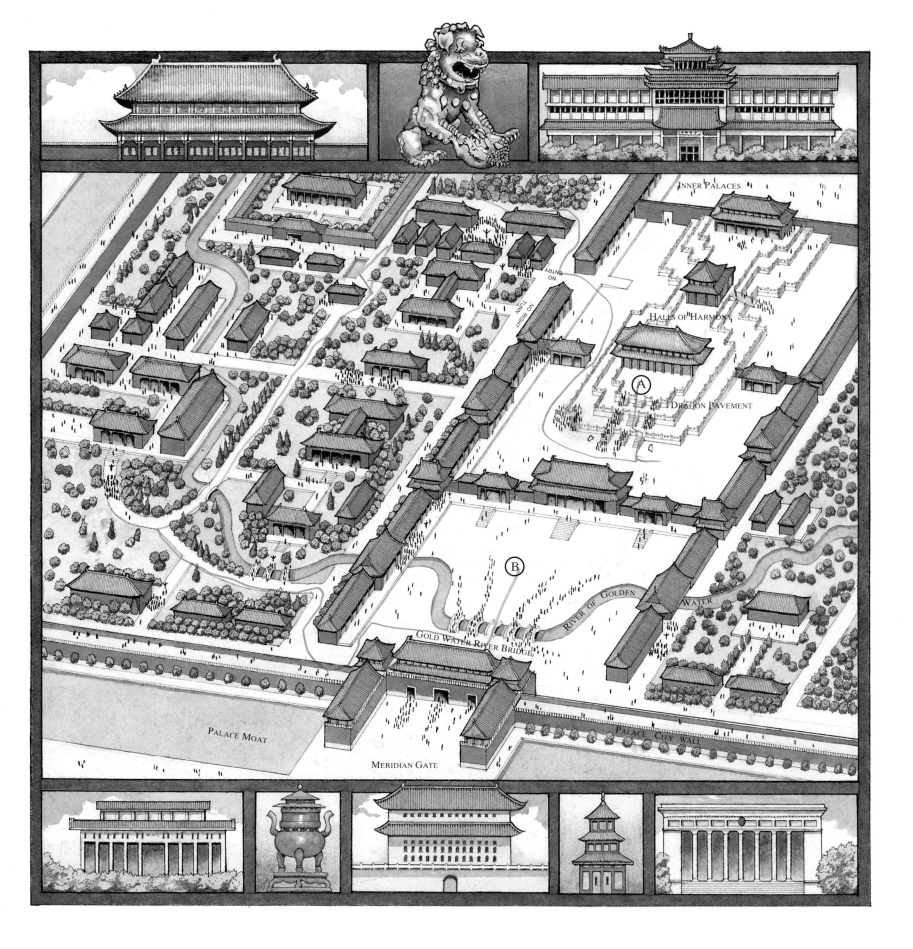

INNER PALACES

HALLS OF HARMONY

Ⓐ

DRAGON PAVEMENT

NO RIGHT TURN

NO ENTRY

Ⓑ

RIVER OF GOLDEN WATER

GOLD WATER RIVER BRIDGE

PALACE MOAT

PALACE CITY WALL

MERIDIAN GATE

SYDNEY • CITY ON THE HARBOR

Sydney, Australia's oldest and largest city and the capital of New South Wales, is a fascinating cosmopolitan center. Straddling the magnificent harbor of Port Jackson, the city was first settled in 1788 as a penal colony. Since then, it has grown rapidly and today is a bustling modern city with a population of more than three and a half million people of over 120 nationalities.

A city of contrasts, Sydney effectively blends early colonial and Victorian sandstone buildings with magnificent modern architecture, such as the Harbour Bridge, Centrepoint Tower, and the Opera House. All of this combined with lush green parks and gardens, sparkling blue waters, a busy thriving port, and world-famous golden beaches makes Sydney an internationally important commercial, cultural, and tourist center. It is impossible to see everything at once, so today we are going to see the famous historic and modern sights in the city center. We are taking a circular tour of this bustling area, from the Conservatorium of Music (**A**) at the Royal Botanical Gardens. Can you find the one clear circular route our tour took?

ROYAL
BOTANIC
GARDENS

BRIDGE STREET

MACQUARIE STREET

KING STREET

YORK STREET

GEORGE STREET

ELIZABETH STREET

COLLEGE STREET

PARK STREET

NO ENTRY

NO LEFT TURN

NO ENTRY

NO ENTRY

RIGHT TURN ONLY

LEFT TURN ONLY

NO ENTRY

LONDON • A ROYAL CITY

The ancient city of London, the capital of the United Kingdom, was founded by the Romans in AD 43. An international center of banking and commerce, London is also home to the British royal family and houses the seat of government. A popular tourist center, thousands of visitors flock to the city from all over the world to see London's cultural heritage: the great buildings, art collections, and museums, as well as the ancient traditions and pageantry, such as the Changing of the Guard at Buckingham Palace. The River Thames, once the main means of transport, snakes through London in elegant, sweeping curves. It is now crossed by numerous road bridges — six between the Houses of Parliament and the Tower of London alone, including the famous Tower Bridge.

Two Americans who have arrived at Victoria (**A**) are to meet some friends at St. James's Palace (**B**). They hail a London taxicab to take them there, and the driver promises to show them some of the famous sights on their way. Can you find the one clear route the taxi driver took?

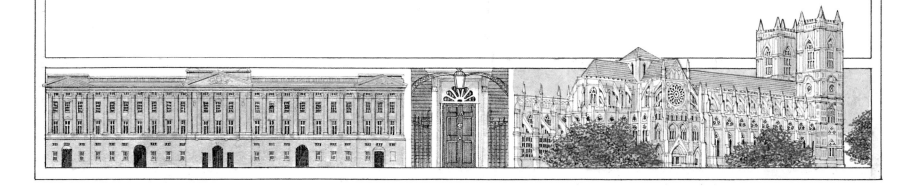

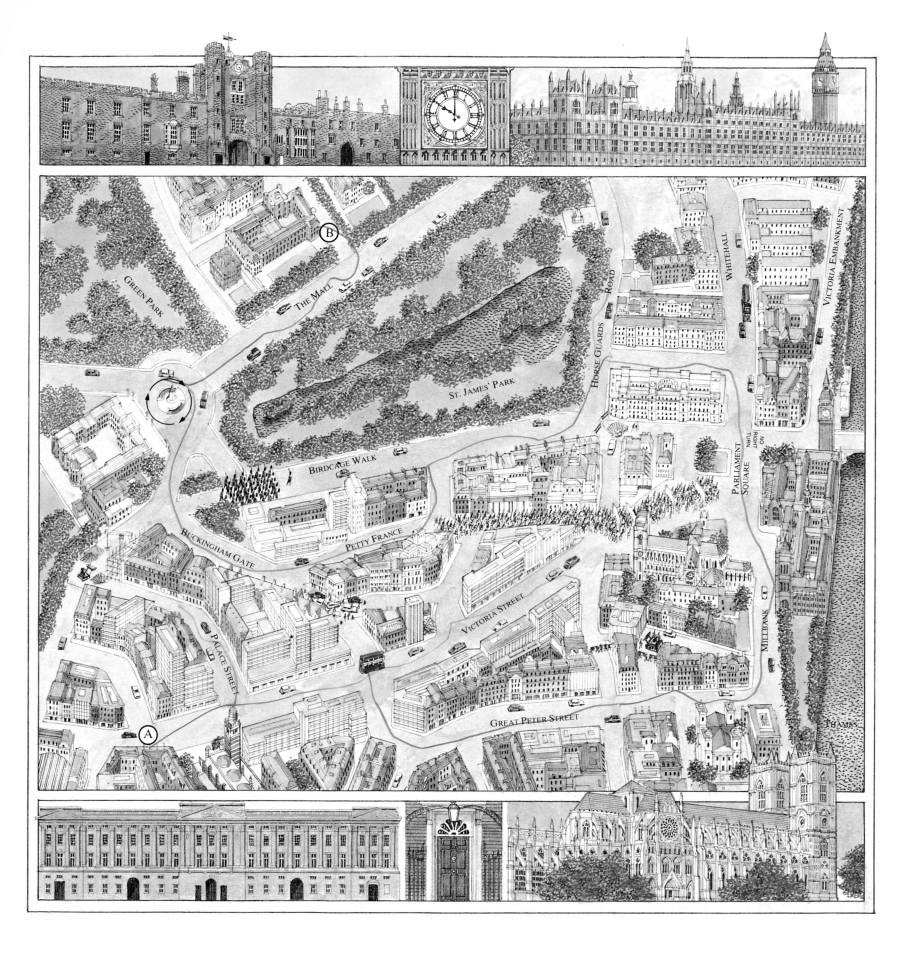

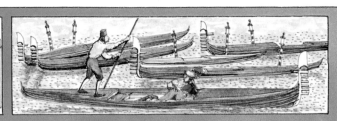

VENICE • THE SERENE CITY

The beautiful city of Venice, *La serenissima* (the most serene), lies
in a crescent-shaped lagoon. The capital of Veneto Province, Venice is one
of Italy's most historic cities. A living museum, this ancient city is renowned
for its canals, fine buildings, and outstanding art galleries that house the
works of many famous Venetian artists such as Titian and Tintoretto.
You can tour Venice by gondola, on any of its 150 or so canals, but perhaps
the best way to see the sights is by walking. Venice is a maze of tiny paths
and passageways. There are many sights of interest to see, but it is
not always easy to find your way to a particular place.
A visitor to Venice decides to walk from the Palazzo Balbi (**A**) to the
Piazza San Marco (**B**) where she can catch a gondola and take a tour via the
Grand Canal. She is surprised to find that the route is more complicated than
she thought. Many of her paths are blocked by construction projects and
parades, while others are dead ends leading nowhere, so she has to make
many detours. Follow the pathways and see if you can find your way from the
Palazzo to the Piazza. But take care, only one pathway takes you there.

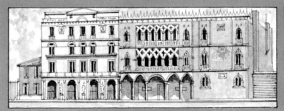

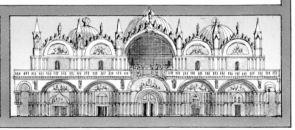

RUGA DEGLI OREFICI

RIALTO BRIDGE

RIO DELLA FAVA

SALIZZADA SAN LIO

MERCERIA SAN SALVATORE

RIO DI SAN SALVADOR

CALLE DEI FABBRI

CANALE GRANDE (GRAND CANAL)

RIO FUSERI

RIO DI SAN LUCA

RIO DEI

BACAROLI

A

CALLE MANDOLA

RIO DELLA VESTE

CALLE DEI FRATI

RIO DI SAN ANGELO

RIO DELLA VERONA

PIAZZA SAN MARCO

B

CALLE LARGA XXII MARZO

LAGOON

PAX TIBI MAR CE

EVAN GELIS TA MEVS

MOSCOW • THE KREMLIN

At the heart of Moscow, the capital of Russia, lies the Kremlin and its famous Red Square. The Kremlin, which means citadel, overlooks the Moskva River, from which the city gets its name. Within the ancient walls of the Kremlin are many magnificent buildings, including the former royal palaces. The glittering onion-shaped domes of the cathedrals that rise above the red-brick walls are a reminder that Moscow has been the center of the Russian Orthodox Church since 1326. A symbol of power and authority, the Kremlin also houses many government buildings, with Lenin's Mausoleum just beyond its walls. The city has expanded greatly since the Communist Revolution in 1917 and is now one of the largest in Europe. Within its boundaries lie 120 museums and galleries and many theaters, including the celebrated Bolshoi Ballet.

We are starting our guided walk of the Kremlin on the banks of the river (**A**). The tour will finish at Spassky Tower (**B**) near St. Basil's Cathedral. From here we can explore the rest of the city. Can you find the one clear pathway our guide took, avoiding all the crowds and obstructions?

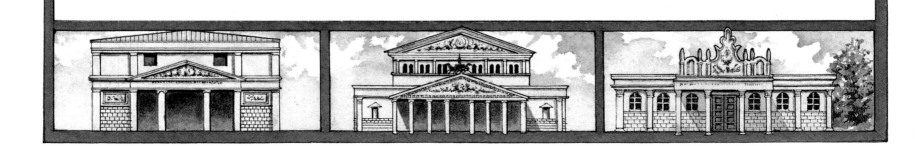

GREAT STONE BRIDGE

BOROVITSKY PLACE

MOSKVA RIVER

MOSKVORETSKY BRIDGE

KREMLOVSKAYA NAB.

ALEXANDROVSKY

MARX PROSPEKT

NO ENTRY

GARDENS

NO ENTRY

NO ENTRY

KRASNAYA PLACE
(RED SQUARE)

OCTOBER 25TH ST.

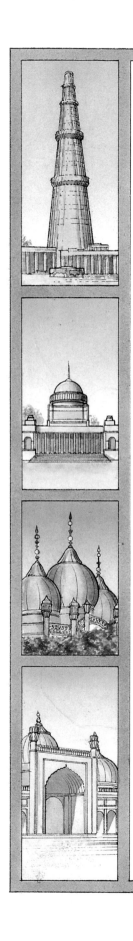

DELHI • THE OLD AND NEW CITIES

Delhi, the capital of India and its third-largest city, consists of two parts: Old and New Delhi. Old Delhi (and for a time, Agra) was the capital of Muslim India between the 12th and 19th centuries. New Delhi is the Imperial City created by the British at the beginning of the 20th century as the capital of India. The two areas could not be more different. Old Delhi centers on the remains of the fascinating 17th-century walled city. With its ancient city gates and narrow winding alleys bustling with activity, as well as the historic Red Fort and beautiful Mogul mosques, one could almost have stepped back in time. In contrast, New Delhi is a spacious open city with wide, tree-lined avenues and elegant modern government buildings designed by the British architect Sir Edwin Lutyens. It is the economic and commercial center of the city. We have been on a tour of new Delhi and have visited some of the ancient sites on the outskirts of Delhi. Now we are going on a circular tour of Old Delhi. The guide has promised us that we will visit all the attractions labeled (1-10) on our map (although not in that order) without going down the same road twice. We have chosen the day of a religious festival, so our route is even more difficult than usual! Can you find the circular tour our party took around Old Delhi starting from Kashmiri Gate (**A**)?

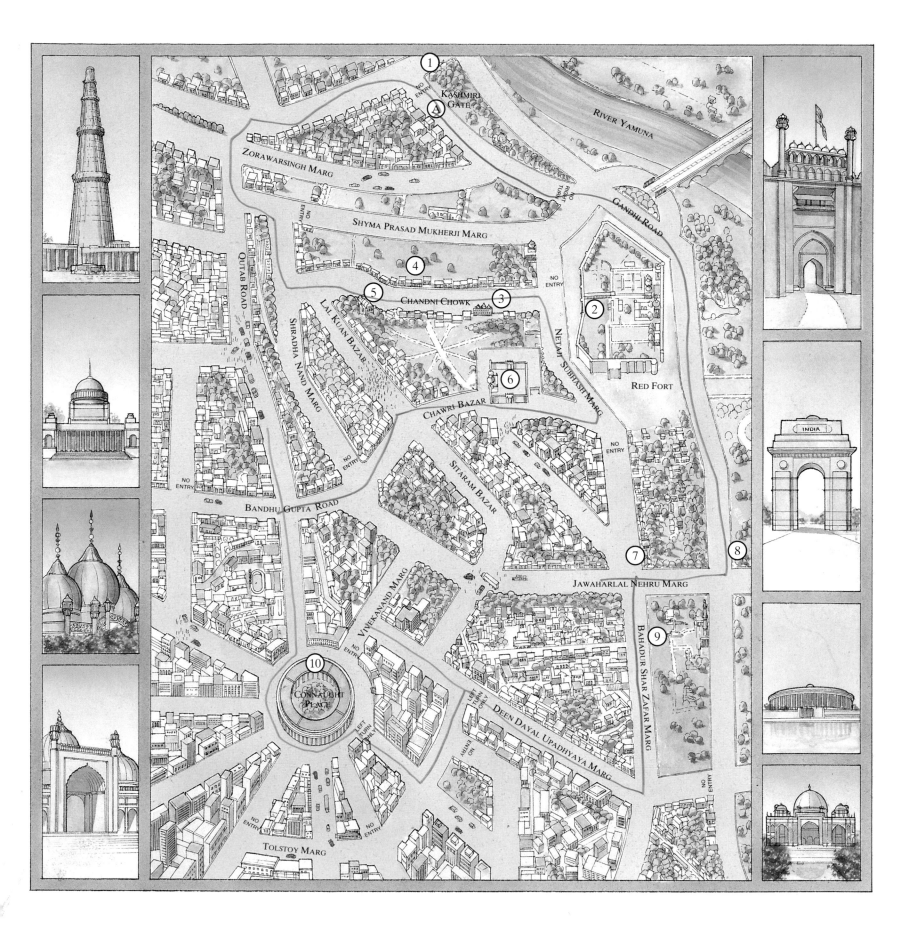

AABB + ABB

MADRID • THE CASTILIAN CAPITAL

Situated in the heart of Spain, on the Castilian plateau, Madrid is Europe's highest capital. A fascinating blend of old and new, the city's architecture varies from the historic glories of the Royal Palace and the Prado Museum to modern cosmopolitan boulevards with stylish shops and lively cafes. Madrid is also renowned for its many beautiful parks and botanical gardens — havens of quiet in this bright, bustling city.

A party of schoolchildren were taken on a special bus tour of the city, starting and finishing at the Plaza de la Independencia (**A**). Unfortunately, they had chosen a festival day for their visit, and so many of the roads were closed. It seemed as if they would not be able to take their tour after all. But the driver knew the city so well that he was able to make a circular tour as promised. Can you find the one clear route that the bus driver took around Madrid?

CALLE DE FUENCARRAL

PLAZA
DE
COLON

GRAN VIA

PLAZA
DE LA
CIBELES

CALLE DEL ARENAL

CALLE DE ALCALÁ

NO
ENTRY

CALLE MAYOR

CARRERA D.S. JERONIMO

NO
LEFT
TURN

NO
ENTRY

Ⓐ

NO
ENTRY

CALLE DE TOLEDO

CALLE DE ATOCHA

NO
ENTRY

NO
LEFT
TURN

CALLE DE ATOCHA

CALLE DE ALFONSO

NO
LEFT
TURN

ISTANBUL • CITY OF TWO CONTINENTS

Istanbul, Turkey's largest city, straddles the Bosphorus at the entrance to the Black Sea. Founded about 660 BC by the Greeks, it is the only city in the world that is built on two continents — Europe and Asia. Formerly known as Byzantium and then Constantinople, Istanbul was the capital of the Byzantine Empire for more than 1,000 years and of the Ottoman Empire for 500 years. The skyline is dominated by the domes and minarets of the ancient mosques that crown and decorate Istanbul's seven hills. A busy, bustling port, Istanbul is a major link between East and West. The city has a wealth of ancient monuments and historic sights, including the Topkapi Palace (once home to the Ottoman Emperors), Hagia Sophia (a Byzantine church), and numerous beautiful domed minarets.

There are so many sights to see that a guided tour is the best way to view this amazing city. A circular tour from the Galata Tower (**A**) will take our tourists past most of the ancient monuments in Old Istanbul. However, the streets are very busy, and a lot of them are one-way systems. Can you trace the only clear circular route that the bus driver took?

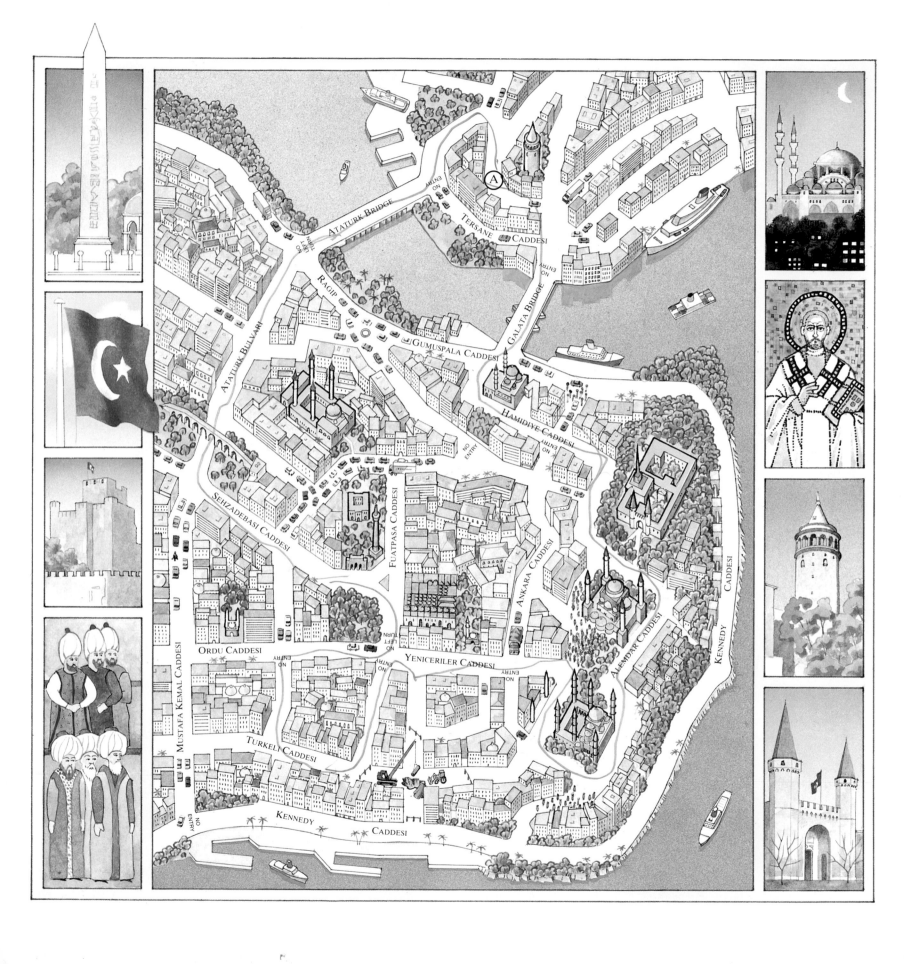

PARIS • CITY OF LIGHT

Paris, the beautiful and romantic capital of France, is world famous for its many galleries, museums, and stunning architecture, as well as its high fashion and marvelous food. From the magnificent romanesque Sacré Coeur to the modern glass edifice of the Pompidou Center, Paris is a city of contrasts. The city itself is quite small — no monument is farther than 6 miles (10 km) from the Notre-Dame Cathedral. Despite this, the number of cars and tourists that flock there to see the sights means that the city center can become difficult to negotiate. Tourists staying at the Hôtel des Marnières (**A**) take a bus tour of some of the sights (1-11) including the Eiffel Tower, the Place de la Concorde, and the Louvre Museum. The bus picks them up at their hotel, and the driver promises them a continuous tour of these famous sights. "We will not go down the same road twice or visit the same building twice," he declares.

The route is not a simple one. Road construction, "no entry" signs, and one-way streets all serve to confuse. Only one route will lead you past all the numbered sites (but not in the numbered order) without going back over your route. Can you find the continuous route that the bus driver took and plot the tour of Paris?

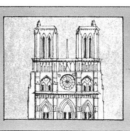
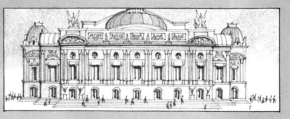

METROPOLITAIN

12

13

14

1

2 PLACE DE LA MADELEINE

FRANKLIN D.

AVENUE DES CHAMPS ELYSÉES

AVENUE GEORGE V

ROND POINT

4

ROOSEVELT

RUE DE RIVOLI

5

6

3

NO ENTRY

AVENUE DE NEW YORK

PLACE DE L'AMA

QUAI DES TUILERIES

RIVER SEINE

NO ENTRY

7

QUAI DU LOUVRE

QUAI BRANLY

PLACE DE LA RESISTANCE

QUAI D'ORSAY

NO LEFT TURN

NO RIGHT TURN

9

11

NO ENTRY

AVENUE BOSQUET

BOULEVARD DE LA TOUR MAUBOURG

10

A

AVENUE DE LA BOURDONNAIS

8

BOULEVARD St. GERMAIN

NO ENTRY

15

16

17

18

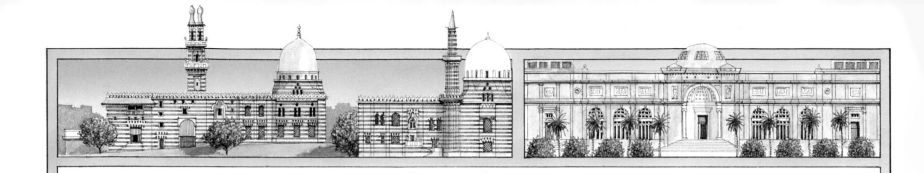

CAIRO • CITY ON THE NILE

Cairo, situated at the head of the mighty River Nile, is shrouded in the splendor and majesty of ancient Egypt. The largest city in Africa, Cairo is an extraordinary mix of ancient cultural treasures and modern skyscrapers. The Egyptian museum, which houses the legendary relics from Tutankhamen's tomb, and beautiful mosques and minarets stand alongside ancient bazaars and ultramodern office blocks. The city streets bustle with activity as cars, buses, and taxis compete noisily with sightseers, street vendors, and livestock of all descriptions. And barely 3 miles (less than 5 km) away, on the city outskirts at Giza, lie the ancient pyramids and the mysterious sphinx.

There is so much for our busy tourists to fit into their day. A friendly guide tells them of a bus tour that leaves from the station (**A**) within the hour. It will take them to Giza, visiting all the famous city sights on the way. Can you find the route the driver had to take around the city and out onto the road to Giza (**B**)?

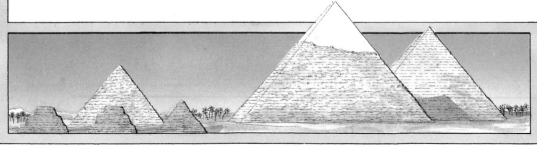

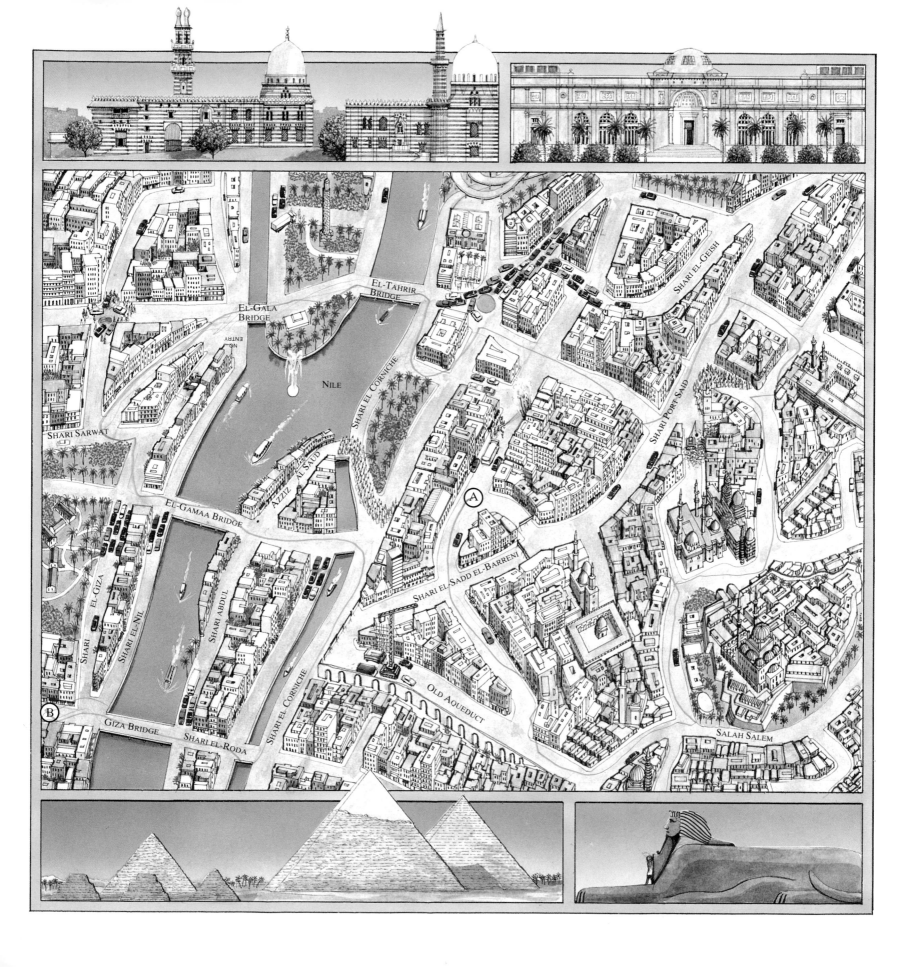

EL-GALA
BRIDGE

EL-TAHRIR
BRIDGE

NO ENTRY

NILE

SHARI EL CORNICHE

SHARI SARWAT

SHARI EL-GEISH

SHARI PORT-SAID

AZZIZ AL SAUD

EL-GAMAA BRIDGE

Ⓐ

SHARI EL-GIZA

SHARI EL-NIL

SHARI ABDUL

SHARI

SHARI EL-SADD EL-BARRENI

Ⓑ

GIZA BRIDGE

SHARI EL-RODA

SHARI EL-CORNICHE

OLD AQUEDUCT

SALAH SALEM

RIO DE JANEIRO • CARNIVAL CITY

Rio de Janeiro, one of the largest tropical cities in the world, is the chief port in Brazil. Discovered by the Portuguese in 1502, Rio was the capital of Brazil from 1763 to 1960. World famous for its dramatic setting, this amazing city perches on a narrow shelf between the mountains and the sea — Guanabara Bay. Rio is a city of sharp contrasts. Magnificent museums, old colonial buildings such as the splendid 18th-century Candelária Church, and beautiful parks stand side by side with skyscrapers, the ultramodern Metropolitan Cathedral, and the largest soccer stadium in the world. Overlooked by the celebrated Sugar Loaf Mountain and Corcovada, Rio's beaches (Copacabana and Ipanema) are among the most spectacular in the world. Fine houses, hotels, and apartments abound, in contrast to huge *favelas*, or shanty towns, that cover the hillsides and house thousands of families.

A group of sightseers is on a tour of the city. Their first stop is central Rio where they are going to visit some of the most famous colonial buildings. The tour starts from the waterfront (**A**) and will take them around this part of the city, then on to some other famous sights. However, it is carnival time, so their driver has to make many detours to miss the crowds as well as other obstacles. Can you find the one clear route the tour took from (**A**) to (**B**)?

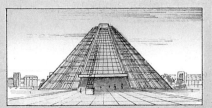

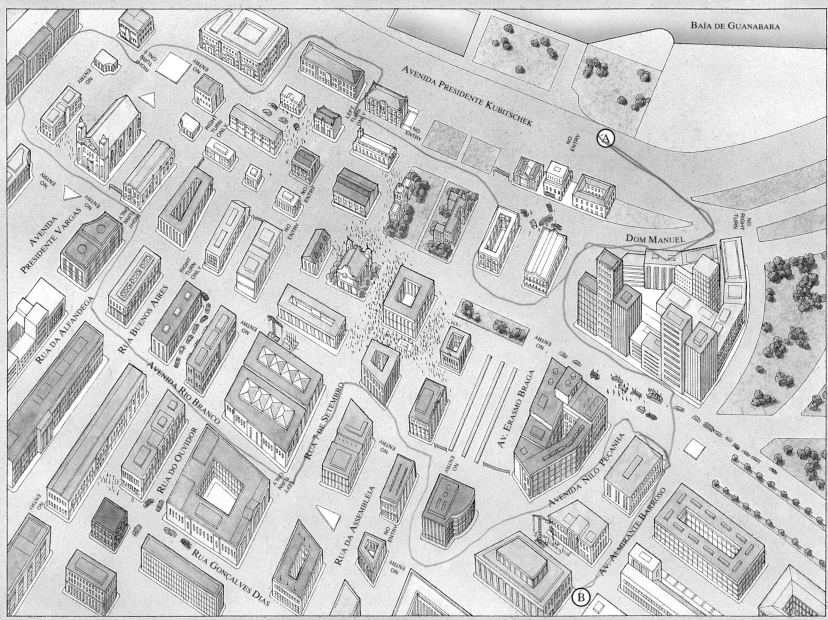

BAÍA DE GUANABARA

AVENIDA PRESIDENTE KUBITSCHEK

NO ENTRY

RIGHT TURN ONLY

NO ENTRY

RIGHT TURN ONLY

LEFT TURN ONLY

NO ENTRY

(A)

NO ENTRY

DOM MANUEL

NO RIGHT TURN

AVENIDA PRESIDENTE VARGAS

NO ENTRY

NO ENTRY

RIGHT TURN ONLY

NO ENTRY

RUA DA ALFANDEGA

RUA BUENOS AIRES

RIGHT TURN ONLY

NO ENTRY

AV. ERASMO BRAGA

NO ENTRY

AVENIDA RIO BRANCO

RUA 7 DE SETEMBRO

AVENIDA NILO PEÇANHA

RUA DO OUVIDOR

LEFT TURN ONLY

NO ENTRY

NO ENTRY

AV. ALMIRANTE BARROSO

NO ENTRY

RUA DA ASSEMBLEIA

NO ENTRY

RUA GONÇALVES DIAS

NO ENTRY

(B)

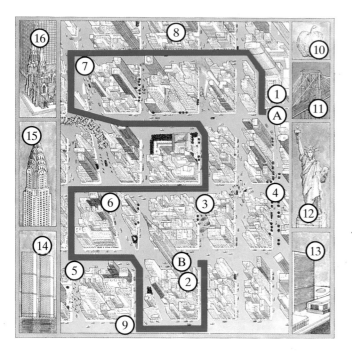

NEW YORK • NEW YORK

New York, a historic city full of dramatic contrasts, has been a busy trading center since the local Algonquian tribes lived there. Originally called New Amsterdam by the Dutch, who bought Manhattan Island in 1626, it was renamed after the Duke of York when the British took control in 1664. After the Revolution, Washington was inaugurated as president at Federal Hall on Wall Street, and New York was the capital from 1789 to 1790. The city has a long list of attractions — so many that at least 18 million people visit it each year. As well as leading the way in fashion and finance, the city has 150 museums, 400 art galleries, 38 Broadway theaters, 87 colleges and universities, more than 800 landmark buildings and interiors, and 51 historic districts. As you find your way from Grand Central Terminal to the Empire State Building, you will pass some of these famous sights.

1. Grand Central Terminal A national monument of American beaux-arts style, Grand Central Terminal was completed in 1913. One of the largest terminals in the world, it has 66 rail lines on the upper level and 57 on the lower level.

2. Empire State Building With 102 floors, 1,860 steps, and a height of 1,250 feet (381 m), the amazing Empire State Building is made from 60,000 tons of steel.

3. Fifth Avenue Fifth Avenue houses many museums, including the Cooper Hewitt, Guggenheim, and Metropolitan Museum of Art. Well known for its luxury department stores, Cartier, Tiffany, and French and Italian boutiques, it is also a shoppers' paradise.

4. Park Avenue Elegant Park Avenue, a combination of business properties and expensive apartments, is a fascinating mix of old and modern buildings.

5. Madison Square Garden This famous stadium seats about 20,000 people.

Madison Square Garden is used for boxing matches and concerts and is home to the New York basketball and hockey teams the "Knicks" and the "Rangers."

6. Broadway Broadway, one of the longest avenues in the world, is famous as the center for smash-hit musicals and plays.

7. Times Square Named after the New York Times building, Times Square is well known for its spectacular New Year's celebration.

8. Rockefeller Center It took eight years (1931–1939) to build the Rockefeller business center. It houses many famous multinational corporations and is a symbol of New York's power and wealth.

9. Sixth Avenue Officially named the Avenue of the Americas, the heraldic symbols of each of the states sometimes hang from flag-poles along Sixth Avenue.

10. The Big Apple The term "Big Apple" originated in the 1920s when it was used by jazz musicians to describe New York.

11. Brooklyn Bridge The Brooklyn Bridge, which connects Brooklyn and Manhattan, was opened in 1883. An amazing feat of engineering with its unusual wire webbing, this 1,595-foot- (485-m-) long bridge is a favorite subject for painters.

12. Statue of Liberty A gift from the French in 1886, the 152-foot- (46-m-) high Statue of Liberty is a symbol of the New World.

13/14. United Nations Building The spectacular United Nations headquarters, designed by 11 architects on a site donated by John D. Rockefeller Jr., was completed in the early 1950s. Another famous skyscraper is the World Trade Center (**14**).

15. Chrysler Building Built in 1930, the glittering top of the Chrysler Building is shaped like the radiator cap on a 1929-model Chrysler car.

16. St. Patrick's Cathedral This beautiful building was modeled after Cologne's Gothic cathedral. St. Patrick's took 21 years to build, from 1858 to 1879.

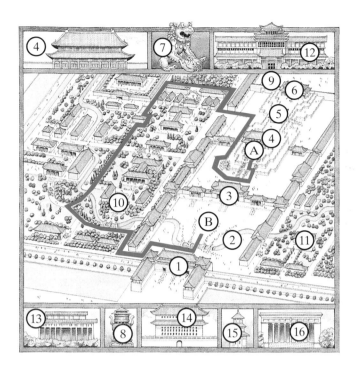

BEIJING • THE FORBIDDEN CITY

Beijing, the capital of China, is a city of great contrasts. It once consisted of two walled (the walls no longer exist) cities, the northern inner city and the southern outer city. Within the inner city lies the old Imperial City, and at its center is the moated Forbidden City, or Gugong, once the home of the Chinese emperors. The city has expanded greatly, and much of the outer city is now a honeycomb of orderly narrow streets and back alleys. Within this bustling industrial center, relics of imperial splendor lie side by side with modern monuments. As you make your way to the inner city toward Tiananmen Square, you will see many historic sights. Once within the Forbidden City, restored by the Communist government as a tribute to the Chinese people, your guide will reveal the wonders of China's imperial past.

1. The Meridian Gate The massive Meridian Gate (Wumen), once the exclusive gateway of the emperors, has one large and two smaller pavilions raised on a marble platform.

2. River of Golden Water The River of Golden Water that flows through the city is spanned by five marble bridges. Only the emperor used the central bridge.

3. Gateway of Supreme Harmony The entrance to a huge courtyard that could hold 100,000 people, the Gateway of Supreme Harmony (Taihemen) is richly decorated with glazed tiles.

4/5/6/7/8. Halls of Harmony The three ornate Halls of Supreme (Taihedian) (**4**), Middle (Zhonghedian) (**5**) and Preserving (Baohedian) (**6**) Harmony with their golden tiled roofs were the center for coronations, New Year's celebrations, and court banquets. The marble stairs and balustrades of the Hall of Supreme Harmony were carved with dragons, the symbol of the emperor. Many buildings were decorated with carvings, and lions (**7**) and huge lanterns (**8**) stood beside the stairways. The Hall of Preserving Harmony houses the fabulous suit of jade and a collection of terracotta warriors.

9. Inner Palaces To the north of the Halls of Harmony, through the Gate of Heavenly Purity (Qianqingmen), lie the inner palaces. The Palace of Heavenly Purity (Qianquinggong), where the emperor presided over affairs of state, is at the center of over forty mansions, libraries, and living quarters.

10/11. Imperial Palaces Other famous halls housing imperial artifacts are the Halls of Military Eminences (Wuyingdian) (**10**) and Literary Glory (Wenhuadian) (**11**).

12. National Art Gallery Built from 1960 to 1962, the National Art Gallery has a renowned collection of modern paintings.

13. Memorial Hall of Chairman Mao Situated in the massive Tiananmen Square, close to the Monument to the People's Hero and the stone sculpture of soldiers and peasants, lies the Memorial Hall of Chairman Mao (Mao Zedong Mausoleum), built in 1977. Here the Communist leader lies in state in a crystal coffin.

14. Gateway to Beijing The massive Beijing Gateway is almost all that remains of the original fortifications of the city.

15. The Temple of Heaven To the south of the palace walls, near the inner city limits, lies the sacred Temple of Heaven (Tiantan). At the entrance is The Imperial Vault of Heaven, which was built about 1530 and is surrounded by the Whispering, or Echo, Wall. The main sacrifices and prayers were held at the white marble Round Altar. The emperor spent the night in the magnificent Hall of Prayer for Good Harvest, with its three-tiered, blue tiled roof and decorative gilding, before returning to the Gugong.

16. Great Hall of the People Built in 1959, the Great Hall of the People in Tiananmen Square is the meeting place for the National People's Congress.

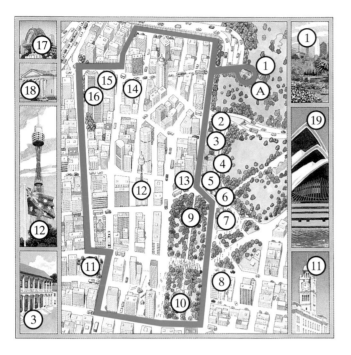

SYDNEY • CITY ON THE HARBOR

Australia's oldest and largest city, Sydney was first settled in 1788 under the leadership of Captain Arthur Philips. He named the colony after the British Home Secretary of the time, First Viscount Sydney. The colony developed into a thriving town between 1810 and 1821, under the governorship of Lachlan Macquarie with the construction of over 200 public buildings and the creation of parks and gardens. He was aided by the convict architect Francis Greenway. Today, Sydney is a cosmopolitan industrial and cultural center covering more than 668 square miles (1,730 km²). The city, famous for its stunning harbor and golden beaches, also has many historic and spectacular modern buildings, such as Centrepoint Tower, the shell-roofed Opera House, and Sydney Harbour Bridge. As you take a circular tour of Central Sydney from the Conservatorium of Music in the Botanical Gardens, you will see some of these fascinating sights.

1. Royal Botanical Gardens Covering over 70 acres (28 ha), the Botanical Gardens contain many native Australian plants and tropical imports. The castle-like 19th century Conservatorium of Music, once the stables for Government House, stands at the entrance.

2. Library of New South Wales Founded in 1826, the State Library houses a vast collection of historic documents.

3. State Parliament House Built in 1810 as a wing to "Rum Hospital," it has been Parliament House since 1829.

4. Sydney Hospital Completed in 1894, the sandstone Sydney Hospital replaced the central block of "Rum Hospital."

5. The Mint Built in 1816 as a wing of "Rum Hospital," it became the Mint in 1851, making coins until 1927. It is now a museum with displays of coins and stamps.

6. Hyde Park Barracks Designed by Francis Greenway, the three-storied sandstone building was completed in 1819. Once used for convicts, it is now a museum.

7. St. Mary's Cathedral Finished in 1882, St. Mary's Catholic Cathedral has beautiful stained-glass windows and mosaic floors.

8. Australian Museum The original 1849 buildings were greatly extended to house the country's largest collection of natural history and cultural displays.

9/10. Hyde Park The 40-acre (16 ha) Hyde Park (**9**) became a formal park in 1810. At the south end is the Anzac War Memorial (**10**).

11. Queen Victoria Building Recently restored, the imposing Queen Victoria building, built in 1898, is now an elegant four-story shopping center. The nearby Town Hall and station, begun in 1868, is topped by a distinctive clock tower. Next door is St. Andrew's, Australia's oldest Cathedral, designed by Edmund Blacket.

12. Sydney Tower The city's most distinctive landmark is Centrepoint and the 1000-foot-(305-m-) high Sydney Tower. The 1981 tower is supported by cables anchored to the roof of Centrepoint. The view from the top takes in the city and harbor.

13. St. James's Church Designed by Francis Greenway, the graceful St. James's Church, built in 1822, is Sydney's oldest church.

14/15/16. Australia Square Sydney has many fine modern buildings, including the Australia Square Tower (**14**), National Bank (**15**) and the Qantas Centre (**16**).

17. Sydney Harbour Bridge Opened to the public in 1932, the Harbour Bridge is the world's widest long-span bridge.

18. Art Gallery The imposing Victorian Art Gallery contains an extensive collection of original Australian art.

19. Sydney Opera House It took 14 years to build the Opera House, which opened in 1973. Designed by Joern Utzon, this stunning building with its tiled sail-like roofs is renowned worldwide.

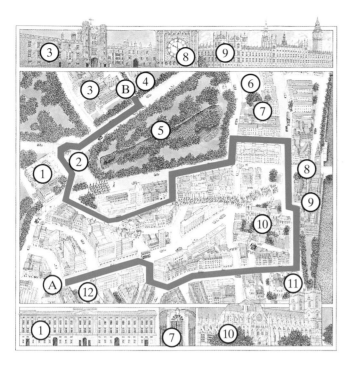

LONDON • A ROYAL CITY

London, the capital of the United Kingdom, is one of the largest capitals in the world. Londinium, the original City of London, was founded by the Romans in AD 43 and covered less than 1 square mile (about 3 km²). Today, this area is the financial center of this vast metropolis. London is famous for its museums, art galleries, and theaters, but perhaps its most popular attraction is the old City of Westminster. Here the tourist can visit historic Royal Palaces, as well as the Houses of Parliament and beautiful parks. And on special occasions, the ancient pageantry associated with this royal city such as the Changing of the Guard or the Trooping of the Colour, can be seen. As you follow the route from Victoria to St. James's Palace, you will pass many of these famous sights.

1. Buckingham Palace Buckingham Palace was built for the Duke of Buckingham in 1705 and bought by George III in 1762. It did not become the main royal home until Queen Victoria's reign in 1837. It was completely redesigned by John Nash in the 1820s, and the present-day front was added by Aston Webb in 1913. The Royal Standard is flown when the Queen is in residence. On most mornings the ceremony of the Changing of the Guard takes place in the palace forecourt.

2. The Queen Victoria Memorial This ornately carved white statue, a monument to Queen Victoria's sixty-year reign, stands in front of Buckingham Palace and at the entrance to Green Park and the Mall.

3. St. James's Palace Built by Henry VIII on the site of an 11th-century hospital, St. James's Palace was the royal home in London from 1698 until 1837. The original buildings, except for the gate tower, were destroyed by fire in 1807. Clarence House, part of the palace complex, is now the home of the Queen Mother.

4. Marlborough House Designed by the famous architect Sir Christopher Wren in 1710, Marlborough House boasts a beautifully ornate hall and staircase decorated with frescoes showing the Duke of Marlborough's battles.

5. St. James's Park Created during the reign of Henry VIII as a deer park, St. James's Park has retained its rural aspect. The central feature is the lake, with its noisy, exotic ducks, geese, and pelicans.

6. Horse Guards Parade Horse Guards Parade lies on the site of the tilt-yard of Whitehall Palace where Henry VIII's knights attended tournaments.

7. Downing Street Named after the 17th-century English statesman Sir George Downing, number 10 is the official home of the prime minister, and number 11 that of the chancellor of the exchequer.

8. Big Ben Big Ben, the 13-ton bell housed in the clock tower of Westminster Palace, was named after Sir Benjamin Hall.

9. Houses of Parliament Once a royal Palace of Westminster, the Houses of Parliament contain the House of Commons and the House of Lords. The medieval buildings, the main royal residence from the 11th to the 16th century, burned down in 1834, except for the Great (Westminster) Hall. The present buildings were rebuilt in the gothic style.

10. Westminster Abbey Dating from 1245, Westminster Abbey houses the magnificent tombs of past kings and queens, including the shrine to Edward the Confessor. English monarchs have been crowned there for centuries. The ornate Coronation Chair was first used in 1307.

11. St. John A typical baroque church, built by Thomas Archer in 1713, St. John stands in the center of Smith Square.

12. Westminster Cathedral Designed by J. F. Bentley and built of striped brick, the 328-foot- (100-m-) tall Campanile of Westminster Cathedral dominates the modern buildings around it.

VENICE • THE SERENE CITY

Venice, founded in the Middle Ages, is an intriguing blend of East and West. More than 150 canals follow the original waterways between the 120 or so islands. The main stream, the Grand Canal, winds through the city and is lined with over 200 palaces, 10 churches, and several other beautiful buildings. The historic center of the city, built on a small group of islets and mud banks, is less than 2 miles (3 km) long and 1 mile (1.5 km) wide. The modern city now embraces the entire lagoon. There are more than 450 palaces and ancient houses, most of which have been built on pilings or stone fill. Venice is also noted for its music and art. Many famous operas were first performed there in the celebrated Teatro La Fenice. The main art museum, the Accademia, lies on the Grand Canal and houses the paintings of prominent Venetian artists. As you find your way from the Palazzo Balbi to the Piazza San Marco, you will pass some of these famous sights.

1. Palazzo Balbi The historic 16th-century Palazzo Balbi was built between 1582 and 1590. It was probably designed by the architect Alessandro Vittoria and is famous for the unusual obelisks on its roof.

2. St. Mark's Square St. Mark's Square (the Piazza San Marco) looks like a large marble room. For centuries it has been the political and social center of Venice. The steps and quay, the Molo, lead inland from its water entrance on the Grand Canal to the patterned pavement of the Little Square (Piazzetta), then into the main piazza.

3. Gondolas Gondolas have apparently been in use since the 11th century, though their present lopsided shape dates from the 17th century. They were once the main form of transport, but now almost every type of vehicle can be seen from large motor boats to water buses.

4. The Doges' Palace The Doges' Palace, once the official home of the Dukes of Venice, was first built about 814. The palace has been badly damaged by fire several times. The present one dates from the 14th century. The imposing "Golden Stair" leads up to the richly decorated chambers of the palace. The Bridge of Sighs, the city's most famous bridge, crosses a small canal that separates the Doges' Palace and the Venetian Republic's prison.

5/6. St. Mark's Basilica The world-famous Basilica (the Cathedral of St. Mark) was completed in 1073. The roofline is decorated with statues and golden Gothic turrets. It has five doorways surmounted by ornate arches and shining domes. Four magnificent gilded bronze horses (**5**), which once pranced above the main doorway, are now housed in the museum.

7. The Lion of St. Mark The symbolic St. Mark's lion of *La serenissima* is seen everywhere in Venice, with and without wings. The main entrance to the Doges' Palace alone has 75!

8. Ca' d'Oro One of the most famous and beautiful of the hundreds of Venetian palaces, the Gothic Ca' d'Oro was built between 1420 and 1440. It is called the Golden House because the decorations on the front of the palace were once gilded.

9. Grand Canal The Grand Canal, the main waterway through the islets, is about 2 miles (3.5 km) long. Over 200 palaces and 10 churches adorn its banks, and at least 46 side canals intercept its course. The 15th-century writer Philippe de Comynes called it "the finest street in the world."

10. Rialto Bridge Until the 19th century, the Rialto Bridge (Ponte di Rialto) was the only bridge to cross the Grand Canal. The present high, single-arched bridge, designed by Antonio da Ponte and built about 1590, is crowded with tiny shops.

11. Campanile The 328-foot- (100-m-) tall red-brick Campanile dominates the Piazza. It was begun in the 9th century but rebuilt in its present form in the 16th century. This commanding landmark, affectionately known as "The Landlord," collapsed in 1902. It was rebuilt "as it was, where it was" on the orders of the Town Council.

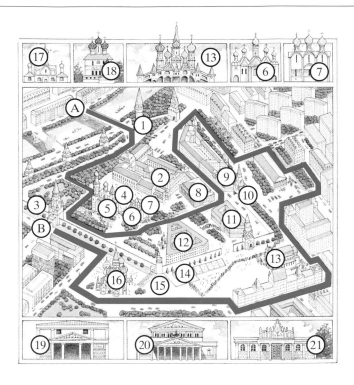

MOSCOW • THE KREMLIN

At the heart of Moscow, the capital city of Russia, lies the Kremlin. This ancient walled citadel with its forts, armories, palaces, and cathedrals was once the czar's enclave. After the Communist Revolution of 1917, it became the seat of government, first of the Soviet State, and now of Russia. Today, many of the buildings are museums, open to the public. Within the Kremlin's walls lie some of Russia's most magnificent buildings, including the former royal palaces and golden-domed cathedrals. Beyond this historic center, Moscow is a modern city, with more than 120 museums, art galleries, and theaters including the famous Bolshoi Theater. As you follow the guided tour around the Kremlin, you will see some of Moscow's famous sights.

1/3/10. Kremlin's Walls The Kremlin's walls form a pentagon over 1 mile (2 km) long, 11 feet to 21 feet (3.5 to 6.5 m) thick and from 16 feet to 62 feet (5 to 19 m) high. There are 19 towers, including the 249-foot- (76-m-) tall Trinity (Troitskaya) Gate (**10**) and Spassky Gate (**3**).

2. The Grand Kremlin Palace This vast complex, once the home of the czars and dating back to the 1500s, houses many treasures. Many of the Grand Palace's 700 rooms have beautiful painted ceilings with columns of marble and granite.

4/5/6/7. Cathedral Square The 14th-century Cathedral Square (Sobornaya Ploshchad) is the most magnificent part of the Kremlin. The paved square is framed by three large cathedrals. The ornate five-domed Cathedral of the Archangel (Arkhangelski Sobor) (**5**) was built in 1505 by the Italian Alevisio Novi. The glittering white Cathedral of the Annunciation (Blagoveshenski Sobor) (**6**), with its nine golden cupolas, dates from the late 1400s. The gilt-domed Assumption Cathedral (Uspensky Sobor) (**7**), built in 1475, houses many rare paintings and the coronation chair of Ivan the Terrible.

8. Palace of Congress This modern glass and aluminium building, built in 1961, is used for international forums.

9. Pleasure Palace The Pleasure (Potieshny) Palace, built in 1650, was later converted into a theater.

11. The Arsenal Constructed by Peter the Great in 1702 for the manufacture of weapons, the Arsenal now houses offices and the Kremlin Guard.

12. The Senate The domed triangular Senate, or Duma, built by Catherine the Great from 1776-88, is now used as offices.

13. History Museum The History Museum, built in 1878, houses over four million exhibits and ten million documents.

14. Lenin's Mausoleum The red basalt tomb of Lenin, built by Shchussev in 1930, once contained Lenin's embalmed body.

15. Red Square Once the political and religious center of the city, Red Square (Krasnaya Ploshchad), is now a major tourist attraction.

16. St. Basil's Cathedral This fairy-tale building with its 187-foot- (57-m-) high central dome, encircled by two tiers each with four brightly colored cupolas, was built by Ivan the Terrible to commemorate Kazan. St. Basil's Cathedral (Khram Vassilia Blazhennovo) is now a museum.

17/18. Churches Many churches in Moscow, such as the 16th-century St. Anne (**17**) and Kolomenskoye Cathedral (**18**) have been restored.

19/21. Monumental Buildings Many of Moscow's older buildings are now offices, such as the Chamber of Commerce, (**19**) or museums like the Education Pavilion (**21**).

20. The Bolshoi Theater The Bolshoi Theater, founded in 1776 and restored in 1856, can seat over 2,000 people.

DELHI • THE OLD AND NEW CITIES

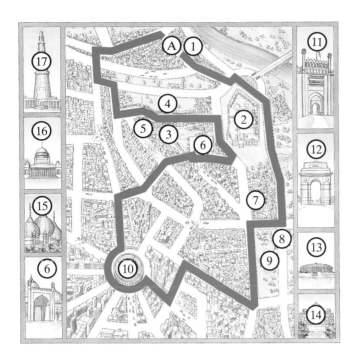

Delhi, the capital of India, is made up of two distinct parts: Old Delhi and New Delhi. Old Delhi is centered around the ancient Muslim city with its crowded, narrow alleys, many beautiful mosques, and the historic Red Fort built by the Mogul emperor Shāh Jahān between 1636 and 1658. New Delhi is a modern city built around the avenue called the Rajpath. 0.5 miles (0.8 km) wide and 3 miles (5 km) long, which leads to the President's residence, once the Viceroy's Palace. Elegant government buildings line the sides of the Rajpath. To the north lies Connaught Place, the link between the old and new, a ring of colonnaded shops, offices, and modern skyscrapers. As you follow the path of the circular tour around Old Delhi down past Connaught Place, you will pass many of these historic monuments.

1/7. City Gates The old city of Delhi was once surrounded by a protective wall with several gates. The Kashmir (Kashmiri) Gate (**1**) was at the northern end of the wall, Delhi gate (**7**) at the eastern.

2/11/15. Red Fort The red sandstone walls of the Red Fort (Lal Qila) (**2**) extend for more than 1 mile (2 km) and vary from 60 feet to 108 feet (18 m to 33 m) high. Dating from the peak of Mogul power, the fort was completed in 1648 by Shāh Jahān. The main gate, the Lahore Gate (**11**), leads into a vaulted arcade. Within the fort are gardens, pavilions, and the Royal Baths. Next to the baths is the beautiful, Pearl Mosque (Moti Masjid) (**15**), built by Aurangzeb in 1659.

3/4/5. Chandni Chowk The main street of old Delhi is the bustling shopping bazaar, Chandni Chowk. There are many historic buildings, including the Sunheri Masjid, Digamber Jain Temple, the kotwali (police station), and town hall. At the west end is the Fatehpuri mosque (**5**), built in 1650 by one of Shāh Jahān's wives. To the north lies the beautiful Mahatma Ghandi Park (**4**).

6. Friday Mosque The Friday Mosque (Jama Masjid), the largest in India, was built in 1656. It has three gateways, four towers, and two 131-foot- (40-m-) high minarets made of alternating strips of white marble and red sandstone.

8. Raj Ghat The Raj Ghat, now a beautiful park, contains a simple black marble platform to mark the spot of Mahatma Ghandi's cremation.

9. Firoz Shah Kotla Built by Firoz Shah Tuglak in 1354, the ruins of Firozabad, an earlier city that Delhi replaced, lie on the border between Old and New Delhi. One famous landmark in the fortress palace is the 43-foot- (13-m-) high Ashoka pillar.

10. Connaught Place Connaught Place, at the northern end of New Delhi, is the business center of the city.

12. India Gate India Gate, a 160-foot- (42-m-) high memorial stone arch, bears the names of 90,000 Indian soldiers who died in World War I.

13. Parliament House An impressive colonnaded circular building, the Indian Parliament House (Sansad Bhavan) is 561 feet (171 m) in diameter and dates from the 1920s.

14. Humayun's Tomb An example of 16th- century Mogul architecture, Humayun's tomb in the south of New Delhi was built by Haji Begum, wife of the second Mogul emperor. Its design was used as the basis for the famous Taj Mahal in Agra.

16. President's Residence Once the Viceroy's house, the palatial President's Residence (Rashtrapati Bhavan) was completed in 1929. This impressive building, designed by British architects, has 340 rooms and an elegant 321-acre (130 hectare) garden.

17. Qutab Minar The buildings in this complex, 9 miles (15 km) south of New Delhi, date from the 12th century. The soaring 239-foot- (73-m-) high tower of the Qutab Minar was started in 1193.

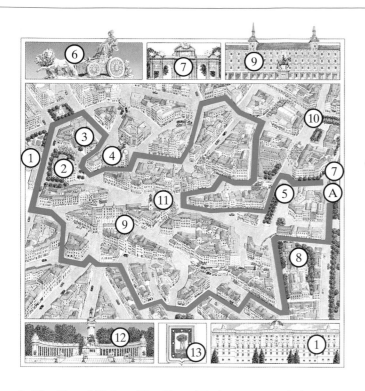

MADRID • THE CASTILIAN CAPITAL

Madrid, the capital of Spain, is situated high on the central Castilian plateau on the River Manzanares. Captured from the Moors in the 11th century by Alfonso VI, it first became Spain's capital under Philip II in the mid-1500s. For centuries, because of its remoteness, there was little building or expansion of the city and the area retained its medieval appearance. However, after the coming of the railroad in the 19th century, Madrid expanded rapidly to become Spain's largest city. Today, it is a fascinating blend of old and new. Madrid is the second-largest industrial center in Spain, as well as being the home of the Spanish royal family and many famous ancient buildings and museums. As you plot the circular tour the bus driver took around the city, you will pass many of these historic monuments.

1. The Royal Palace The Royal Palace (Palacio Real), also called the Palacio de Oriente (Palace of the East), stands on the site of the original Moorish fortress. The present palace, with its Corinthian columns, dates from 1738. It has many richly decorated chambers, over 2,000 rooms in all, and houses priceless art collections.

2. The Royal Theatre The first performance at the Royal Theatre (Teatro Real), built between 1818 and 1850, was Donizetti's "La Favorita."

3. The Convent of the Incarnation Founded in 1611 by Margaret of Austria, the Convent of the Incarnation (Convento de la Encarnacion) houses many famous paintings and religious relics.

4. The Convent of Descalzas Reales The Convento de Descalzas Reales, or Royal Barefoot Sisters, now occupied by Franciscan nuns, dates from 1570. The historic buildings house many artistic treasures, including several tapestries. The shrine of the convent church has many religious relics and jewels.

5/6. Cibeles Square The fountain and goddess Cibeles at the center of Cibeles Square (Plaza de la Cibeles), completed in 1792, were commissioned by King Charles III. The Communications Palace (**6**), (Palacio de Communicaciones), a huge post office opened in 1918, lies at the end of the square.

7. Gateway of Alcalá The Gateway of Alcalá (Puerta de Alcalá), a monumental stone archway with white sculptured figures built by Charles III, stands in the center of Independence Square (Plaza de la Independencia).

8. Prado Museum Built for Charles III, the neoclassical Prado Museum (Museo del Prado) is now an art gallery housing some of the finest works of Velazquez, Goya, El Greco, Titian, and Bosch.

9. Main Square Finished in 1619, the Main Square (Plaza Mayor) has nine arched entrances and a bronze statue of Philip III at its center. Until recent times this was the scene of pageants and bullfights.

10. Colón Square The spacious Colón Square (Plaza de Colón) has many new public buildings, and the city airport terminal operates far below ground. In the center of the square is a statue of Christopher Columbus and a monument to the discovery of the New World.

11. Gateway of the Sun A busy meeting point of ten streets, the Gateway of the Sun (Puerta del Sol) houses the old post office (1768) whose clock gives Spain its official time. The original gate, part of the ancient town wall, no longer exists. It was torn down in 1570.

12. Retiro Park Retiro Park (Parque del Retiro) is famous for its beautiful gardens and sculptures, particularly the statue of Alfonso XII.

13. City Crest The city crest pictures the monument of the bear and tree that stands before the Gateway of the Sun.

ISTANBUL • CITY OF TWO CONTINENTS

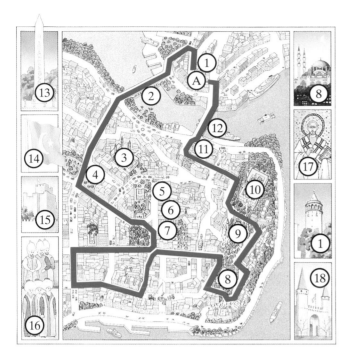

Istanbul, Turkey's largest city, is unique — it is the only city built on two continents: Europe and Asia. Founded in about 660 BC by the Romans, it was known as Byzantium and was the capital of the Byzantine Empire for more than 1,000 years. Later it became the capital of the Ottoman Empire and was renamed Constantinople. Today, Istanbul is a bustling port, but the ancient monuments have been restored and preserved, and the Golden Horn is an oasis of past civilizations. As you take a circular tour of old Istanbul, you will see many ancient wonders, some dating from the days of the Roman Empire. From the ancient, walled Topkapi Palace, the former home of the Ottoman Emperors, to the many beautiful domed mosques with their towering minarets, Istanbul is a fascinating blend of old and new, East and West.

1. Galata Tower The Galata Tower, built in 1348 as a watchtower, has a spectacular view across the Golden Horn to old Istanbul.

2/12. Atatürk and Galata Bridges The swollen waters of the Golden Horn are crossed by many bridges, including the Atatürk (**2**) and Galata (Karakoy) (**12**).

3. Süleymaniye Mosque The beautiful domed mosque of Suleyman the Magnificent is the finest work of the 16th-century architect Mimar Koca Sinan. In the forecourt lie the tombs of Suleyman and his favorite wife Roxanne.

4. Aqueduct of Valens About half a mile of the 4th-century Aqueduct of Valens still survives. It towers 66 feet (20 m) above the Atatürk Bulvari.

5/6. Istanbul University Once the Ministry of War, Istanbul University (**5**) was built in 1870. Within its grounds lies the 295-foot- (90-m-) high Bayezit Tower (**6**), built in 1823 for fire-watch duty.

7. Grand Bazaar This famous bazaar (Kapali Carsi), founded in the 1450s is a small city within itself. The largest covered market in the world, it houses 4,000 shops under one roof.

8. Blue Mosque The majestic Blue Mosque (Sultan Ahmet), built in 1609 for the Ottoman Sultan Ahmed I, is unique – it has six minarets. Blue-tinted light reflected from more than 20,000 Iznik tiles gives this beautiful mosque its popular name. The mosque has particularly beautiful ceilings and also houses a rare collection of ancient, handwoven rugs and carpets.

9/17. Hagia Sophia One of the greatest monuments of Byzantium, the beautiful domed church of St. Sophia (Hagia Sophia) was rebuilt in the 6th century by Emperor Justinian. Some 900 years later, it was converted into a mosque, and four minarets were added. It is now a museum housing many intricate carvings and paintings, as well as the world-famous glitteringly detailed murals and mosaics, such as this of St. Chrysostome (**17**).

10/16/18. Topkapi Palace The main entrance to the walled citylike complex of the Topkapi Palace (**10**), once the home of the Ottoman Emperors, is Bab-i Humayun gate (**18**). The palace, which consists of many courtyards and splendid buildings, is now a museum packed with rare jewel and porcelain collections, as well as many religious relics and royal treasures. The recently restored Museum of the Orient houses a unique collection of Turkish and Islamic art, including 15th-century paintings of royal ceremonies (**16**).

11. Yeni Mosque The Yeni Mosque has a peaceful, tiled courtyard with a brightly colored arched roof.

13. Obelisk The obelisk, which is inscribed with Egyptian hieroglyphics, was brought from Egypt by the Emperor Theodosius.

14/15. Istanbul Castle Istanbul Castle (Anadolu Hisar) (**15**), built to defend and control the straits in 1393, stands on the banks of the Bosphorous. The Turkish flag (**14**) flies from the square turret.

PARIS • CITY OF LIGHT

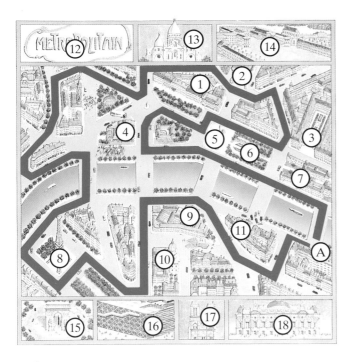

Paris was founded more than 2,000 years ago on the Île de la Cité. For centuries it has been a center of art and culture as well as being world famous for its high fashion and food. Its title — City of Light — arose during the Age of Enlightenment in the 17th and 18th centuries. It is still true today, for Paris remains a center of education and learning. The historical center is based around the Seine. The Île de la Cité, with the famous Notre-Dame, was the seat of religion and government. The left bank was traditionally the center of learning and the right bank the business center. The many ancient buildings, monuments, gardens, and wide avenues make Paris one of the most beautiful cities in Europe. As you find which route the bus took on its tour of Paris, you will see some of these famous sights.

1. Élysée Palace Built in 1718, and once the home of Madamme de Pompadour, the Élysée is now the president's official home.

2. Ste. Marie-Madeleine The church of Ste. Marie-Madeleine, modeled after the Pantheon in Athens, looks like a Greek temple.

3. Palais-Royal Willed to the royal family by Cardinal de Richelieu, the Palais-Royal now houses the Council of State.

4. Grand Palace The Grand and Little (Petit) Palaces, built for the World Fair of 1900, now exhibit art collections.

5. Place de la Concorde The view from the Arc de Triomphe du Carrousel (**15**), built in 1808 for Napoleon I, up through the Place to the Arc de Triomphe, is unique. The Obelisk, a gift from the viceroy of Egypt, once stood in the Temple of Luxor.

6. Tuileries Gardens Designed by Le Nôtre for Louis XIV, the Tuileries are a splendid example of French formal gardens.

7. Louvre Built in the 1400s as a fortress to protect Paris, the Louvre became the world's largest palace. It is now a museum.

8. Eiffel Tower Once the tallest building in the world at 984 feet (300 m), this famous tower was built by Gustave Eiffel in 1889 for the World Fair.

9. Bourbon Palace Seized by the people during the Revolution, the Bourbon Palace now houses the National Assembly.

10. Hotel des Invalides The Hotel des Invalides was built by Louis XIV to shelter 7,000 old or invalid soldiers. The gold-domed church of St. Louis houses the tomb of Napoleon.

11. D'Orsay Museum Once a railway station, the D'Orsay now houses an impressionist art collection, including Monet and Van Gogh.

12. Métropolitain The Métro, a subway, carries millions of passengers daily.

13. The Sacré-Coeur This beautiful domed church, the Sacré-Coeur, is perched high above Paris in the district of Montmartre, which is famous for its artists and clubs.

14. Palace of Versailles Built in the 1600s just outside Paris by Louis XIV, the Palace of Versailles has many apartments, vast gardens, and splendid fountains.

15. Arc de Triomphe A memorial to Napoleon's victories, the Arc de Triomphe houses the Tomb of the Unknown Soldier.

16. Pompidou Centre Ultramodern, with transparent escalators, the Pompidou is a center for the arts and a huge library.

17. Notre-Dame A Gothic cathedral, the Notre-Dame was built between 1163 and 1345. Damaged during the French Revolution, it was restored in the 1850s. Napoleon was crowned there in 1804.

18. The Opéra Designed by Charles Garnier in 1862, the Opéra has a lavish baroque decor of colored marble. Chagall repainted the ceiling in 1964.

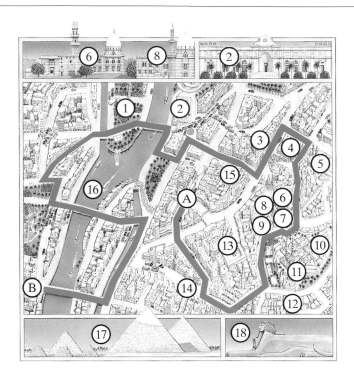

CAIRO • CITY ON THE NILE

Cairo (El Qahira), the capital of Egypt, is situated on the banks of the Nile at the crossroads between the East and the West. Founded on the Arabic city of El Fustat, which dates from AD 641, Cairo is now an extraordinary blend of the old and new. The largest city in Africa, it is the cultural and business center of Egypt. New Cairo is a modern working city of broad avenues and modern buildings that gives way to Old Cairo with its mosques and ancient bazaars. Within the ancient 12th-century citadel and its precincts lie many beautiful mosques, some dating back to AD 800–900. At El-Giza, just a few miles south of the city, are the pharaoh's burial pyramids and the ancient sphinx. As you follow the route around the city, then out on to the road to Giza, you will see some of these famous monuments.

1. Cairo Tower An emblem of the modern city, the 614-foot (187-m) Cairo Tower (El-Borg) has observation towers from which there are panoramic views of the city.

2. Egyptian Museum The world's finest and largest collection of Egyptian antiques, including the treasures of Tutankhamen, is housed in the Egyptian Museum.

3. Museum of Islamic Art Founded by the German architect and scholar Franz Pasha, the Museum of Islamic Art houses masterpieces from every Islamic country.

4. El-Muayyad Mosque Muayyad Mosque, built between 1405 and 1410, is also known as El-Ahmar, the "Red Mosque." The sanctuary has a beautiful painted wooden ceiling. The bronze gate at the entrance came from the Sultan Hasan Mosque.

5–9. Ancient Mosques Cairo is famous for its beautiful mosques, including the splendid El-Hazhar (**5**), which was completed in AD 972 and given the status of a university by Caliph El-Aziz, the Quani Bey Medresse (**6**), and Mahmoudiya (**7**). The El-Rifai Mosque (**8**) was built in 1912. The resplendent Sultan Hasan Mosque (**9**), built in 1363 for Sultan Hasan el-Nasir, has the tallest minaret in Cairo (180 feet [55 m]).

10. Citadel Situated at the foot of the Moqattam Hills, the Citadel was begun by Saladin in 1176 using stone from the pyramids at Giza. The only remains of the original structure are the outer walls.

11. Mohammed Ali Mosque Often called the Alabaster Mosque, the Mohammed Ali Mosque, one of the city's greatest landmarks with its tall, extremely slender minarets and ornate domes, was completed in 1857.

12. Necropolis The cemeteries and necropolises house the tombs of many famous people, including those of the Mamelukes and Caliphs, which date back to the 11th and 12th century.

13. Ibn Tulun Mosque Built from AD 876-879, Ibn Tulun Mosque is the second oldest in Cairo. Its 131-foot- (40-m-) high minaret in the forecourt was modeled on those of the Great Mosque of Samarra on the Tigris.

14. Old Aqueduct This Islamic aqueduct stretches for about 31 miles (50 km).

15. Abdin Palace Now the home of the Egyptian president, the 19th-century Abdin Palace once belonged to the king. The former royal apartments are now a museum.

16. River Nile The longest river in the world, the River Nile's annual floodwaters have supported farming on its fertile floodplains for thousands of years.

17. Pyramids of Giza Built about 2600-2500 BC, the pyramids at Giza housed the tombs of the ancient pharaohs.

18. Sphinx The Great Sphinx at Giza, built between 3000 and 2500 BC, guards the tombs of the pharaohs. Weathering and vandalism caused great damage, but the majestic figure has recently been restored.

RIO DE JANEIRO • CARNIVAL CITY

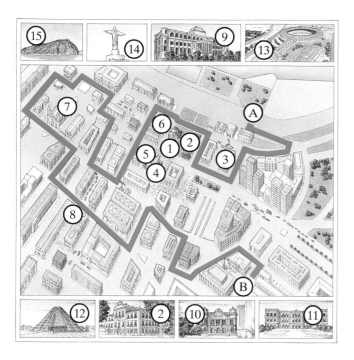

Discovered by the Portuguese in 1502, Rio de Janeiro soon became one of Brazil's largest settlements. In the 18th century, Rio grew rapidly and became a stronghold of the Portuguese empire. Beautiful churches and royal palaces were built, many of which still survive today, and for a time the Portuguese royal family ruled here. The city spread rapidly between the steep hills and the ocean. In 1889, after Brazil became a republic, Rio developed into a modern capital city. It remained the capital until 1960 when Brasilia, the new capital, was built. Present-day Rio is a spectacular metropolis – one of the world's largest tropical cities with more than eleven million people. Famous for its fine buildings, silver beaches and colorful carnivals, Rio is a vibrant port and an important commercial center. As you follow the tour around central Rio, you will see its modern face as well as its colonial past.

1. November 15 Square The historic November 15 Square (Praça XV de Novembro) is named after the day in 1889 when Brazil became a republic. The square has many historic buildings and monuments, including a statue of King João VI, a beautiful fountain, built in 1789, and the stately Teles Arch (Arco de Teles).

2. Viceroy's Palace This elegant three-storied building, the former residence of the Portuguese viceroys, was completed in 1743. Today, the Viceroy's Palace (Palácio dos Vice-Reis) is a museum.

3. Naval Museum The Naval Museum (Museu Naval e Oceanográfico) has a fine collection of model ships and guns.

4/5/6. Ancient Churches Opposite the square lies the 18th-century baroque Carmo Church (Igreja de Nossa Senhora do Carmo) (**4**), the former cathedral in which the emperor of Brazil was crowned. Next door is the Church of Our Lady of Mount Carmel (Igreja de N. Sa. do Monte do Carmo) (**5**). Its interior has richly decorated walls and fine marble sculptures by Mestre Valentim. Nearby is the pretty 18th-century Lapa Merchants' Church (Igreja de N. Sa. de Lapa dos Mercadores) (**6**).

7. Pius X Square Within Pius X Square (Praça Pio X) lies the beautiful Candelária Church (Igreja de N. Sa. de Candelária). Built from about 1775 to 1810, the interior is decorated with colorful marble.

8/9/10. Avenida Rio Branco The city's main street, originally called Avenida Central and renamed in 1912 after the Baron of Rio Branco, has Portuguese-style mosaic pavements. There are many fine buildings on the Avenida Rio Branco (**8**) including the beautiful National Library (Biblioteca Nacional) (**9**) the most important in Brazil, which houses more than three million books, the Municipal Theater (**10**), and the Fine Arts Museum.

11. National Museum Founded in 1818 by King João VI, the National Museum (Museu Nacional) is one of the oldest scientific centers in South America. The impressive three-storied building was the former Imperial Palace.

12. Metropolitan Cathedral The ultramodern Metropolitan Cathedral (Catedral Metropolitana) is made of reinforced concrete with enormous stained-glass windows that flood the interior with sunlight. The large nave can accommodate 20,000 standing people.

13. Maracanã Stadium Built for the World Cup in 1950, the impressive Maracanã Stadium is the biggest soccer stadium in the world, housing up to 200,000 fans.

14. Christ the Redeemer The statue of Christ the Redeemer (Cristo Redentor) with arms stretched out over the bay, stands on top of the 2310-foot- (704-m-) high Corcovado peak. The 100-foot- (32-m-) tall statue, designed by Paul Landowski, is a national monument.

15. Sugar Loaf From the 1296-foot (395-m) summit of the Sugar Loaf (Pão de Acúcar) there is a spectacular view over Rio.